REA

FRIENDS
OF ACL

3 1833 04818 93

D0876985

African Americans and College Choice

MAY 1 2 2000

African Americans and College Choice

The Influence of Family and School

Kassie Freeman

Foreword by M. Christopher Brown II

STATE UNIVERSITY OF NEW YORK PRESS

Published by
State University of New York Press, Albany

© 2005 State University of New York

All rights reserved

Printed in the United States of America

No part of this book may be used or reproduced in any manner
whatsoever without written permission. No part of this book may be
stored in a retrieval system or transmitted in any form or by any means
including electronic, electrostatic, magnetic tape, mechanical,
photocopying, recording, or otherwise without the prior permission
in writing of the publisher.

For information, address State University of New York Press,
90 State Street, Suite 700, Albany, NY 12207

Production by Marilyn P. Semerad
Marketing by Anne M. Valentine

Library of Congress Cataloging-in-Publication Data

Freeman, Kassie.
    African Americans and college choice : the influence of family and
    school / Kassie Freeman ; foreword by M. Christopher Brown II.
        p. cm.
    Includes bibliographical references and index.
    ISBN 0–7914–6191–2 (hardcover : alk. paper) — ISBN 0–7914–6192–0
    (pbk. : alk. paper)
1. African Americans—Education (Higher) 2. College choice—Social
aspects—United States. 3. Education, Higher—Parent participation—
United States. I. Title.

LC2781.P74 2004
378.1′9829′96073—dc22

                                                                    2004016080

                    10 9 8 7 6 5 4 3 2 1

In honor and memory of my mother,
Lauretta Wilson Freeman

CONTENTS

ILLUSTRATIONS

Foreword

M. Christopher Brown II

Accolades, Annotations, and Assessments

Kassie Freeman's book *African Americans and College Choice: The Influence of Family and School* marks a paradigm shift in the investigation of two areas of scholarly inquiry—college choice and African American students. The general contention has been that all students bring the same schematic processes to the college selection and attendance process. The accepted belief in the academic research community has long been that students are provided with information from sundry sources and in myriad formats that predispose them to attend college or not, influence which institution they select, and precondition their attrition or completion. The scholarly community conceded one differentiator: the earlier one is exposed to the sundry sources or myriad formats the greater the likelihood of college attendance and completion. These pseudouniversal findings led the federal government to enact the "Gaining Early Awareness and Readiness for Undergraduate Programs" (GEAR UP) initiative.

Not in contradiction to the established research literature, but in a departure from the blinding or blinded universality of the research literature, Freeman explains the significant role of families and schools in African American students' college choice decision. The acknowledgement of families and schools centers on the students' predisposition toward college rather than the decision to attend a specific college. Freeman's break with the corpus of researchers in the college choice arena coincides with an increasing scholarship on the various forms of capital (that is, human, cultural, social, and economic) operating in and around school settings. Consequently, this new interpretation of the college choice process should not be viewed as a radical repulsion from accepted thinking, but as a refreshing, innovative, and accurate accounting of a significant group of students whose experiences have been silenced. Please note that this silencing was more than likely not intentional on the part of prior researchers, but the natural homogenization that occurs when disparate data (especially outliers) are drawn to the line of regression.

Interestingly enough, Comer and Poussaint (1992) explored the issue of college adjustment for African American students and other youth. Their research evidenced the social, cultural, and contextual differences that African American youth experience in and around the collegiate span. They further noted the importance of family and community structure as buffer zones for negative encounters. However, there is no treatment of the role of these buffers in influencing and facilitating African American student college attendance.

Further, *African Americans and College Choice* brings the empirical research community and the "mother wit" and collective knowledge of the African American community together (Brown & Davis, 2000). There is some consensus that the family, church, and school form a trinity within the historic African American corporate experience in the United States. The logic goes that the African American family is the fount from which educational development and epigenetic transformations occur. This home life extended to community congregations like the church.

The church furthered the intellectual development of African American youth through Sabbath or Sunday schools and pageants that required recitation and quantification (Anderson, 1988). The import of the church extended into two branches. First, the African American religious congregations became a significant founder of and to the extent possible funder of schools, institutes, and colleges designed for the education of Black children (Brown, 1999, 2002). Even to this day, the denominational affiliations persist for a number of historically Black colleges and universities. Second, the Sunday school programming was often conducted by persons who also served as teachers in the local schools and area colleges (Anderson, 1988; Walker, 1996).

The third part to the trinity of institutions with educational impact is the schools attended by African American children. These schools were historically segregated by law, and today remain relatively homogenous due to resegregation or economic diameters of the school attendance circumference. The intellectual foresight to explore the nexus between schools and families is most apropos. The role of the church is also an important influence on African American students' postsecondary choice process.

Nevertheless, Freeman has redefined the center of the college choice discourse, particularly, as it relates to African American students. Her findings actually also threaten to recenter the research practice of utilizing familial demographics (that is, socioeconomic status) as a statistical predictor. It is abundantly clear that the importance of whether a student's parents attended and graduated from college is dwarfed by the index on whether the parents value, promote, and emphasize college attendance. Lewis (1997) writes, "The black family is traditionally achievement-oriented, especially as this relates to high expectations for education" (p. 26). Further, Ray Stannard Baker wrote in his book, *Following the Color Line*, "The eagerness of the [African American] people for a chance to send their children to schools is something astonishing and pathetic. They will submit to all sorts of inconveniences in order that their children may get an education" (as quoted in Anderson, 1988, p. 283).

I fear that the dominoes will not stop with the import for the research community's investigations of family influences. Throughout her book, *Their Highest Potential* (but particularly in chapters 5 and 6), Vanessa Siddle Walker (1996) explores the role of school settings and personnel in supporting African American college attendance. These expectations were conveyed through formal and informal mediums with a high component of expectation. Likewise and even more so, Freeman demonstrates how school personnel impact African American student college choice. This confirmatory data serves to reinvigorate scholarship on self-fulfilling prophecy, resiliency, and power in school settings, especially those settings populated by the underserved, underrepresented, underresourced, and undervalued (Brown, 2000; Delpit, 1995; Feagin, Vera, & Imani, 1996).

In sum, Feagin, Vera, and Imani (1996) proffer:

> African Americans place a heavy emphasis on education because of its role in family and community. Education is about a liberated future that must be better than the oppressive past. Pressing

hard for higher education for children today is linked to the
strong educational aspirations of African Americans in the dis-
tant and recent past. The prospect of a successful future for
one's children and grandchildren helps to justify and give dis-
tinctive meaning to the collective suffering and struggles of the
past and the present. In many ways, black parents do not differ
from other parents who work hard to put their children through
college. However, for black parents the education of their children gives meaning to their struggle against racism as well as to
other aspects of their individual and familial histories. . . . The
familial pressure is common to many American families, but it
takes on an added dimension for those who are members of an
oppressed group that has faced major racial barriers to education. (pp. 22–23)

There is an ominous undertone in the above that offers a com-
pelling backdrop for *African Americans and College Choice*. Families and schools not only care about, but conjoin in the lifelong
educational success of African American students. In fact, as Freeman has announced, they are the primary influences in the predisposition of African American students' aspiration to, selection of,
matriculation through, and completion of college.

Moving from Regurgitations of Literature
toward Policy and Praxis

There is no question that "the family is the first and most
important center of orientation for all children. How 'family' is
defined is the point of reference from which we can determine
the extent to which the needs of children can be met" (Morgan,
1995, p. 205). However, until now, there were questions about
what differentiated African American student pipeline data from
other investigated populations (Brown & Bartee, 2000). The
unique contexts and factors surrounding any population (for
example, immigrants) encountering American educational struc-
tures warrants serious and unconfounded investigation. The challenge is to move from predetermined and often dated research
toward a contemporary corpus of scholarship that addresses both
the phenomenological and pragmatic considerations for schools
and their students.

In their book *Going to College* (1999), Hossler, Schmit, and Vesper investigate the social, economic, and educational factors that influence student decision making. However, they do not singularly address the role of families and schools in influencing college choice. The *Going to College* model focuses on the student as the primary decider in the college choice equation. Freeman's *African Americans and College Choice* makes clear that the African American family (including its communal members) and community schools play a major role in African American college choice. Freeman does not deconstruct the Hossler-Schmit-Vesper equation, but rather adds a new subequation to their first additive—aspiration. While enumerating the components of aspiration, Freeman concomitantly extends and renames this plank of the college choice research predisposition. She explains that predisposition is a correlative of aspiration; hence you cannot have one without the other. *African Americans and College Choice* makes visible the schematic influences that structure the metacognitive ways in which African American students decide whether to attend college and secondarily which institution. In a long overdue and bracing encore to the already thorough analysis, Freeman investigates whether a Black college campus or other institutional type is selected. Further, she posits the reasons why institutional choices are often made (especially for high-achieving African American students). The treatment of historically Black colleges is particularly noteworthy. Freeman's analysis includes these institutions as equal and acceptable options in the postsecondary school selection process.

The findings and analyses from the volume have significant implications for whether and how African American high school graduates transition to the collegiate level. The text answers three critical questions: (1) What are the background characteristics of college-bound African American students? (2) Who and what are the influences on African American high school students' college choices? (3) What challenges and opportunities do colleges face in recruiting African American students? Answering these fundamental questions and their endemic offspring will aid educators, policymakers, and researchers in facilitating academic success for all students, particularly African Americans students.

The question that faces academia remains "How do schools work?" (deMarrais & LeCompte, 1998). Supplementing the investigation of familial roles and functions, Freeman explicates the core role of schools in the decision to attend college. I will say what she does not say: many schools serve as factors for African American student attrition rather than completion. Certainly, I concede that there are social, familial, and often intellectual factors that contribute to African American student exhaustion and abandonment of school settings. However, research cannot divorce the school culture, climate, curriculum, and composition (that is, staffing) from their significant though undocumented role in disrupting the African American student's educational pipeline (Brown & Bartee, 2000). What Freeman does is to name the place and opportunities in which school settings have been proven to influence student predisposition toward college attendance. Respectfully, she scantly alludes to the sociological axes upon which schools operate (race, class, and geography). I will place a period behind this point to maintain the respectful tenor with which she addressesd so divisive an issue. However, it behooves me to quote de Castell and Bryson (1997): "[R]esituating questions about educational interventions firmly within a politics of identity contests dominant narratives about educational progress" (p. 6).

Freeman's volume is replete with new and innovative conceptual frameworks. The visual application of the theoretical and research connections via conceptual maps, diagrams, and models that demonstrate how the various subjects and variables interact one with another offers more than any text could detail. There is no doubt that these visual enablements will be highly cited, replicated, challenged, and analyzed in subsequent scholarship. Most worthy of note is Freeman's final model, which illuminates the African American student's choice process as different from others. Freeman's Model of Predetermination explores the roles of family and kinship (including fictive kin), school characteristics, student cultural characteristics, and college predetermination in the collegiate participation of African American students.

The final deduction from Freeman is that schools can be either positive or negative influences in the African American student's college choice process. The researcher, educator, or policymaker's hope becomes the "new possibilities for theory and practice that emerge when it is no longer assumed that education and schooling are overlapping processes for Africans in societies in which multiple cultures exist and unequal power relations sustain a hegemonic racial order among the members" (Shujaa, 1994, p. 342). There is a clarion invitation at the close of the text to create and invent, explore and discover, as well as research and write about new ways to positively utilize schools in the promotion of college choice.

I do not believe that Freeman nor her readers are naïve enough to believe that the transformation and the promotion of schools as harbingers of African American college choice will metamorphically occur with the closing of the book. However, what Freeman has done is given us the research data that is required, along with the conceptual maps for envisioning, developing, and implementing fundamental educational change. In *Other People's Children*, Lisa Delpit (1995) reminds us of the aspects embedded in school settings that comprise the educational "culture of power." Delpit names the codes and rules that enable some and disenable others. *African Americans and College Choice* provides explicit and relevant findings that can effectuate a neutralization of privilege and an equitable negotiation of educational access, opportunity, and outcomes as they relate to college choice.

After the Foreword

In 1960, W. E. B. DuBois spoke prophetically about postsegregated schooling in America. He warned educators that several ominous trends would result. He said, "[African American] teachers will become rarer and in many cases will disappear. [African American] children will be instructed in public schools and taught under unpleasant if not discouraging circumstances. Even more largely than today they will fall out of school, cease to enter high school, and fewer and fewer will go to college" (Aptheker, 1973, p. 151). His premonition has come true. There are meaningful differences in the school experiences of African American students in primary, secondary, and collegiate settings. Kassie Freeman's book, is a seminal work on reducing those differences through college predisposition, attendance, and completion.

I close with the words of Watkins, Lewis, and Chou (2001) in *Race and Education*. They declare that "equitably shared, advanced technology and the creation of great wealth can reconfigure the world, improving the lives of all. If not, the continuation of racism, ignorance, privilege, and greed will condemn us all" (p. xii). The future of African American students, you, and me are fundamentally linked to the egalitarian concept of equity through education. At best, we all stand to benefit; at worst, we are doomed to a society undone by ignorance, desperation, and paranoia. I choose education.

Preface

The research on African Americans in every facet of higher education is sorely lacking, from their decision-making process as to whether or not to participate in higher education to their actual participation in the graduate school pipeline. While there is much researchers know in general about the college choice process (the decision to participate in higher education, the search for an institution, and the selection of an institution), there is still much to learn about the decision-making process of underrepresented groups, such as African Americans. The following are among the many unanswered questions:

(1) Are the influences on the students' decision process the same for different cultural groups?

(2) At what age or grade does the process of choosing higher education begin?

(3) What role does economics really play in the decision process for groups such as African Americans?

(4) What role does the secondary school attended play in the college choice process of African Americans?

(5) What role does cultural affinity play in the decision process for African Americans selecting a higher education institution type—that is, Historically Black Colleges and Universities (HBCUs) or Predominately White Institutions (PWIs)?

Among the researchers who focus on college choice, it is generally agreed that the decision process of not only whether or not to participate in higher education but also of which institution to choose falls into three phases: (1) predisposition, (2) search, and (3) choice (Hossler & Gallagher, 1987; Stage & Hossler, 1989). In the first phase (predisposition), students determine whether or not to go to college; in the second stage (search), students and their families begin to investigate various higher education institutions; and in the third stage (choice), students begin to narrow their options of higher education

institutions and make a final decision about which college or
university to attend.

This book almost exclusively focuses on the first stage, predisposition, or what I refer to as "predetermination," that is, circumstances that often determine which students, or even whether
students, will choose to go to college. It is important to better
understand the influences on African American students' postsecondary education decision-making process and how the decision
process differs among African American students. To learn about
how young African Americans plan their postsecondary futures, I
conducted and taped a series of group interviews with students in
grades 10 through 12 in both public and private schools in
Atlanta, Chicago, Los Angeles, New York, and Washington, D.C.
Those cities were chosen because they have large African American populations as well as the highest incomes and lowest poverty
rates among African Americans, meaning that students in those
cities are more likely to consider attending college. In all, sixteen
group interviews with seventy students were conducted. In order
to encourage free expression regarding perceived barriers to
higher education, I asked open-ended questions about why some
African American students seem uninterested in college. (See the
appendix for the profile of the sample and the research methods).

I was struck by the similarity in the responses given by students across schools and geographic areas, allowing me to draw
some clear conclusions about the difficulties African American students face in planning their paths after high school. Transcripts
from the interviews will expose those problems and possible solutions to them in the students' own voices. (Note that the names of
teachers and counselors have been changed in the transcripts).

Moving away from the predisposition stage, chapter 8
explores the choice phase and broadly examines influences on
African Americans' consideration of institution type (that is,
whether to attend an HBCU or a PWI). Since HBCUs are rarely
included in research, this chapter provides some clues as to the
allurement of these institutions. Understanding the choice process
of African Americans holds great importance for higher education
administrators for the purposes of recruitment, admissions, and
retention. In order to increase the overall enrollment of African

Americans in colleges and universities, it is useful to understand the influences on their decision process. As for retention, academic and social integration are more easily achieved if educators have a better understanding of how students make their decisions in the first place.

There is still reason for great concern about African Americans' participation in higher education. According to Hearn, Griswold, Marine, and McFarland (1995), understanding African Americans' decision process to continue beyond secondary schooling is "momentous and merits serious attention" (p. 1). Previous researchers have not given a voice to African American students, who are in the best place to assess the problems and judge programs that have been most beneficial to them or their peers in terms of influences on their choice process. By all accounts, college choice for African American high school students is a complicated process that necessarily has to take into consideration the context of their culture. Otherwise, any solutions might possibly be based on models that do not fit the circumstances of these students. It is obvious that current models are not working to the degree that they should to increase African American college attendance; therefore, it is critical that educators and policymakers better understand what Affican American students have to say about what they perceive has worked for them and will work for others like themselves based on their experiences.

There are several books on African American issues in higher education. However, these books, such as the ones written by Nettles (1988), Gurin and Epps (1975), Allen and Epps (1991), and Fleming (1984), are specific to different aspects of African American experiences within higher education institutions. Since, surprisingly, virtually no books have been written on the topic of African Americans and college choice, this book is a necessary addition to the literature. Using the stories of a sampling of students and weaving their voices into the research literature can provide a unique contribution to educators and policymakers on African American high school students and the choice process.

Hopefully, this book will also be useful for those conducting research on African Americans' participation in higher education. The entire research area on the aspirations and motivations of

African Americans is terribly underinvestigated, and this book seeks to add a much-needed cultural aspect to the literature. Also, this book should be of interest to elementary and secondary school administrators, teachers, and counselors, since it addresses issues related to programs and models that will be useful to increasing aspirations and motivations of African American students at different stages of their development. Policymakers who have typically modeled programs to increase the desire of African Americans to pursue postsecondary education on the majority population will also find this book useful.

This book focuses on several aspects of African Americans' decision to participate in higher education. It is divided into three parts: (1) familial and individual influences, (2) school influences, and (3) putting the puzzle together. More specifically, in part 1, chapter 1 focuses on the role of family and individual influences; chapter 2 investigates at what age or grade the decision process begins; chapter 3 examines how male and female students approach the choice process; and chapter 4 reviews economic influences on African American students' decision process. The chapters in part 2 examine school-related influences. Chapter 5 assesses curriculum influences; chapter 6 reviews the influence of channeling; chapter 7 examines the characteristics of different high school types that are successful in channeling their students; and chapter 8 ends part 2 with an exploration of the selection of higher education types (HBCU or PWI). In part 3, chapter 9 gives suggestions from the students themselves about what models they believe researchers need to use to address the choice process for African Americans. Finally, chapter 10 emphasizes the need for cultural characteristics to be an integral part of the research and programming on African Americans and college choice.

In order to set this research in context, the book begins with an examination of the puzzle of African American students' stated aspirations and their actual participation in higher education. The question, then, is: What are the missing parts of the puzzle? It is important to explore this puzzle to better understand the necessity for such a book. Also, the examination of this puzzle provides an overview of college choice theory that undergirds this research. In this way, the chapters can almost exclusively be used for the voices of the students, and their voices can be interwoven into the literature. The concluding thoughts in part 3 will provide details about the implications of this research—putting the pieces of the puzzle together.

Acknowledgments

I want to sincerely thank Professors Walter Allen of the University of California at Los Angeles, Robert Crowson of Vanderbilt University, Terrence E. Deal of the University of Southern California, and James Hearn of Vanderbilt University, without whose confidence in my ideas and research this book never would have been possible. They each, in different but very important ways, have provided me inspiration, encouragement, guidance, and support.

To the schools that so graciously allowed their students to participate in this study, I am extremely grateful. However, it is to the many African American students who spoke so openly and honestly that I shall forever be indebted. Through their voices, I became much more aware of the importance and special responsibility of being a researcher.

I am very grateful to the Spencer Foundation for the funding that allowed me to collect the database for this study. Being able to hear the rich and different stories of African American students would not have been possible without the support of the foundation.

Finally, Debra Walters, editor extraordinaire, deserves all the credit for making these chapters into a book. Through our work together, she has been a personal and professional motivator. I am blessed to have found her. However, Margaret Copeley, copyeditor, deserves the credit for finalizing the details of this book.

INTRODUCTION

The Puzzle of College Aspirations versus Attendance

African Americans have always placed a high premium on education, believing it to be the one commodity that could empower them. African American sociologist Billingsley (1992) writes that "the thirst for learning like the thirst for family life crossed the Atlantic with the African captives" (p. 174). That very fact makes it even more puzzlling, then, that on the one hand, African Americans have consistently been found to have higher educational aspirations than other groups—particularly when background variables are held constant (Hearn, 1991; Orfield et al., 1984; St. John, 1991)—but on the other hand, their aspirations have not always translated into higher education participation.

Researchers Hearn, Griswold, Marine, and McFarland (1995) have explored an aspect of the puzzle in their study titled *Dreams Realized and Dreams Deferred*. Their findings, in effect, continue to support the reality of the "disjunction between expectations and attainment of Black students" (p. 13). Other researchers (e.g., Thomas, 1980) have made similar findings.

However, while most researchers and policymakers seem to acknowledge the existence of this puzzle, instead of trying to explore more deeply the meaning of such a paradox in order to build on the high aspirations of these students to attend college, they seem to accept the notion put forth by St. John (1991): "Presumably, Blacks have higher post-secondary aspirations than other applicants with similar test scores and high school experiences. Thus, while high aspirations improve the probability that Black and low-income students will attend college, having high aspirations alone does not guarantee their college attendance" (p. 153). In other words, while there is acknowledgment that African Americans have high aspirations and that their aspirations do not translate into college attendance, researchers have tended to ignore why this is the case and have failed to develop ways to change this pattern.

Closing the gap between aspiration and participation in higher education for African American students is particularly important since educators and economists are in agreement on the importance of increasing their college attendance. More specifically, Simms (1995) has discussed the direct relationship between African Americans' postsecondary education and their economic success.

If aspirations are "wishes or desires expressing an individual's hopes about the future" (Chapman, 1981, p. 494), intuitively, it would seem that in order to increase the participation of African Americans in higher education it would be imperative to better understand the disjunction between their hopes about the value of education and their actual participation. Better understanding this puzzle could explain for policymakers and researchers why it has been difficult to increase African American college attendance to an acceptable level.

The intent of this book is to search for pieces of the puzzle. What do we know about the overall relationship between aspirations and participation, particularly as it relates to African Americans' decision process to attend college? What are the missing links between these students' aspirations and actual participation? How can better understanding this relationship inform policymaking, particularly as it relates to increasing African Americans' college attendance?

The Puzzle

Discussions of aspiration and decision making relative to attending college generally focus on cultural and social capital and economic and financial capital (Hossler, Braxton, & Coopersmith,

1989). However, Orfield et al. (1984) conducted a comprehensive study of access and choice in higher education in Chicago which concluded that minorities are channeled into college based on defined geographic locations—where they live. While most choice theorists would include the concept of channeling—a concept that is greatly underexamined—under the cultural and social models of decision making, it is considered separately in this book.

The sociological model of student choice (which is the umbrella model for cultural and social capital), at least as described by Hossler, Braxton, and Coopersmith (1989), focuses on the factors which influence aspiration. This model describes the family socioeconomic level and student academic ability as predictors of students' aspiration for college. It is noteworthy, however, that in a study where the socioeconomic status was held constant, African Americans were more likely than Whites to begin some college (Olivas, cited in Orfield et al., 1984). Hossler, Braxton, and Coopersmith (1989) also indicated that expectations from others, such as parents, teachers, and friends, also influence students' aspiration to participate in higher education. According to Orfield et al. (1984), next to socioeconomic status, the secondary school attended is the primary structure that provides access to college. It is the school curriculum (academic versus technical-vocational), counseling (regarding college availability and preparation), and grading that have a tremendous impact on students' choice as to whether or not to go to college.

However, if it is the case, as some theorists (Bourdieu & Passeron, 1977; Coleman, 1988, 1990; Collins, 1979) have suggested, that postsecondary aspiration and high school academic decision making grow out of the cultural and social capital of families, it seems logical that aspiration and choice are culturally based and will not necessarily be based on societal (elite) values. It is ironic that models to increase aspiration have generally been based on society at large, completely ignoring the culture of each group, in this case African Americans.

In addition to cultural and social capital as major rationales for how students choose college participation, the econometric model and financial capital have also been postulated as explanations in the decision process (Anderson & Hearn, 1992; Hossler, Braxton, & Coopersmith, 1989; Orfield et al., 1984). In the econometric model, as these theorists and economics of education theorists (e.g., Becker, 1975; Cohn, 1979; Johns, Morphet, & Alexander, 1983; Thurow, 1972) have suggested, expected costs and future earnings expected from attending college are the primary considerations for students' perception of the value of higher education, although economic status, race, and education of parents may have a bearing on future earning potential.

The notion of future earning potential as it relates to African American students' pursuit of higher education has been a greatly underexplored topic. For example, Barnes (1992) completed a study on African American twelfth-grade male stay-ins (those who were persisting through high school), and, regarding those students' economic goals, she found the following: "It is interesting that 43.7% indicated they wanted to become wealthy or comfortable rather than identify an occupation" (p. 96).

Socioeconomic factors such as parental income level and occupation, educational level, and number of siblings are also posited as indicators of students' choice regarding college participation (Alwin & Otto, 1977; Anderson & Hearn, 1992; Boyle, 1966; Hossler & Gallagher, 1987). Parental income and educational level have both a direct and an indirect effect on college choice. Indirectly, the lower the parental income level and education, the less information the parents will have available to assist their children with financial decision making. Directly, Orfield et al. (1984) stated it this way: "Family income is viewed as causing inequalities in educational access" (p. 30). As an example, "because family income is much lower for minority students than for White students, the former are three to four times more dependent on federal financial aid than the latter" (Morris, cited in Orfield et al., 1984, p. 25). While research is replete with information about the impact that the lack of financial aid has on college attendance (Cross & Astin, 1981; Nettles, 1988), what is increasingly clear is that there is a void in understanding how different cultural groups interpret or perceive the expectations of future earnings in making their postsecondary education plans.

The most puzzling aspect of how African Americans differ in choosing whether or not to continue their studies after high school is the gap between their aspirations to attend college and actual attendance. Many college choice theorists have written about this paradox without explaining it (Hearn, 1991; St. John, 1991;

Thomas, 1980). Research literature abounds with what Mickelson (1990) calls the "paradox of consistently positive attitudes toward education, coupled with frequently poor academic achievement" (p. 44) among African Americans.

In order to further the understanding of this paradox, Mickelson (1990) offers the best description of forces that might prevent African American students from acting on their aspirations. She divides the attitudes toward schooling into two categories: "abstract attitudes, which embody the Protestant ethic's promise of schooling as a vehicle for success and upward mobility; and concrete attitudes, which reflect the diverse empirical realities that people experience with respect to returns on education from the opportunity structure" (p. 45). In her opinion, students' realities vary according to their perceptions and understanding of how adults who are significant in their lives receive more equitable or less equitable wages, jobs, and promotions relative to their educational credentials. Since, according to this notion, students are influenced by their perceptions which shape their realities, light is shed on how African American students can aspire to participate in higher education but can believe that actually doing so might not be economically viable.

Missing Pieces of the Puzzle

Assessing the missing pieces of the puzzle between aspiration and participation in higher education (that is, the steps in the decision-making process that create the void between beliefs and actuality) is paramount to both bridging the gap in research and developing workable programs and models that go beyond "This is just the way it is." This is particularly important if, as Mickelson (1990) and Ogbu (1978) have indicated, individuals act on what they perceive and not necessarily on what research says is reality. While research has not dealt with this void in any appreciable way, what can be pieced together as missing links in research in better comprehending the aspiration and actual participation of African Americans is a more in-depth understanding of two categories: family and individual factors, and school factors.

Additionally, African American students need to have a voice which will be heard and taken seriously by administrators and educators. Perceived psychological barriers and absent voices present the greatest challenge to closing the gap between aspirations and participation. African Americans' perceived psychological barriers have to be better understood and examined in greater detail. In fact, African American high school students, when asked to identify perceived barriers to participation in higher education, name not only economic barriers, but also psychological barriers such as "loss of hope," "college was never an option," and the "intimidation factor" (Freeman, 1997). In order to better understand the depth of the meaning of these barriers to African American students, their voices surely have to be heard. In this study, I conclude that it is important not only for researchers to include individuals as subjects in their studies, but to include their voices in the development of solutions to their problems. Otherwise, individuals might not buy into participation in programs. The college choice process has typically been evaluated in quantitative terms. Rarely, if ever, have studies assessed what the quantitative findings mean from the perspective of different groups. There will always be a gap between perception and reality if individuals do not have a say in the definition of their reality.

Overall, what research has indicated and continues to indicate is that there are missing parts of the puzzle between what the data tell us and what African Americans do, particularly as it relates to choosing to go to college. In order to continue to increase African American college attendance, a major piece of the puzzle has to be added: programs at the elementary and secondary school level must be culture specific. As Ogbu (1988) has indicated, the historical and structural aspects of a culture have to be considered. Each culture has a different frame of reference; therefore, understanding how different groups give meaning to their realities is crucial to the success of any program development.

In summary, each of the missing pieces of the puzzle as to why African Americans' aspirations do not often translate into higher education has to be researched in greater depth. Like any puzzle, if a part is missing the whole picture cannot be seen. Consequently, for policymaking, an incomplete puzzle could make it difficult to develop sustainable, workable programs and models.

This book examines, from the perspectives of African American students, the influences on the decision process that leads them to choose to go to college or not. This book is merely the beginning of putting the pieces of the puzzle together to gain a better understanding of those influences and to develop workable programs and models to increase the number of those students who attend college. There is much more work to be done.

Part One
Familial and Individual Influences

3 1833 04818 9390

CHAPTER 1

The Influence of Family

Wrongly, African American families are often accused of not being involved or interested in the outcome or the educational process of their children. Whether it is participating in a Parent Teacher Association (PTA) meeting at the elementary and secondary level or assisting students in the transition to higher education institutions, African American parents are depicted as uncaring. In fact, a whole body of literature has sprung up to demonstrate the linkages between community and school, often targeting African American children as not being successful because their parents are not actively participating in the activities of the school.

While no one would doubt or question the importance of parental involvement in the schooling process, the findings regarding many African Americans' participation are often skewed or distorted. Many prominent African American historians and sociologists who have written about the African American family have discussed the belief of these families in the role and power of education (Anderson, 1988; Billingsley, 1992; Franklin & Lightfoot, 1989). Perhaps the more recent assessment of findings related to a lack of African American family involvement in their children's schooling points to both a lack of understanding as to how the African American family interprets its role and involvement and a conflict between the values of the family and the school. Vernon Feagans (1997) discusses some of these conflicts, such as style of

11

punishment, in her book, *The Perils of School: Cultural Clashes in Communities and Classroom.*

While some may argue that it is not essential to understand the content of the debate surrounding the involvement of African American parents in their children's schooling in elementary and secondary schools to understand college choice, I would suggest that it is crucial to do so because college choice theorists recognize the hugely important role that the family plays in influencing students' postsecondary plans (Hossler & Gallagher, 1987; Hossler, Braxton, & Coopersmith, 1989). The questions underlying both debates, although often unspoken and unwritten, are: Do African American families value education? Do they perceive a return on their investment in higher education? If so, how do they impart this value of education to their children, that is, do their children perceive the same value? In order to understand the context of how African American families influence the college choice process of their children, it is important to first review the value that these families have placed on education over time and in what ways they have passed on their value of education, particularly higher education, to their children. Without such a context, it is difficult to understand the African American family's role in the college choice process.

Overview of African American Families' Belief in Education

Sociologist Billingsley (1992) addressed the quest of African Americans for education often through his writings. As he indicates, "Education is the traditional opportunity through which Black families find their place in life. And having found it, they replicate their experience again and again through their children" (p. 172). Education, in the broadest sense, is fundamental to being able to communicate and to participate in the affairs of society. When any group of people has been denied the right to read and write, as was historically the case with African Americans when their ancestors came to this country, instinctively, they will come to attach a high premium on those skills (Anderson, 1988).

First of all, early on African Americans recognized that they were locked out of the flow of information—there was no way they could adequately navigate their surroundings without the